After all this Time

Ashwath Narayan

INDIA • SINGAPORE • MALAYSIA

ISBN 979-8-89446-564-7

Also by the author

The Sun, Moon, Mars, & The Stars

After (H)ours

Maladaptive Coping Mechanisms

Insignificant Other

Archetype for Destruction

Big Feelings

Contents

Part II: Progress

Part I: Regression

How Odd

How odd
That love should remain
After the harrowing hurt and pain
Of betrayal and broken promises
Have ebbed away

How odd
That love should remain
After so long

How odd
That love should remain
Even though you are gone

How odd
That the *presence* of love
Is pain unfathomable

How odd

To wish that love be gone

Heartbreak is Humbling

Heartbreak is humbling

Humbling because

It showed me

How little control I have

Over my body

And even though

My head understands

My body cannot seem to reconcile

My muscles ache

More pain than I've known before

My stomach cramps

And I clutch it and roll up into a ball on the floor

And my chest

Oh, my chest

Crushing, excruciating, asphyxiating

My heart rebels, revolts against my mind

While to my heart, I try to be kind

Safe

My three dogs are rescues

With histories of trauma and abuse

And though they are seniors

Living out their final years

They are puppies

Still plagued by their own demons and fears

And sometimes on walks

They startle and freeze

Petrified by some sight or sound

From the street

And I hug them

Hold their heads close to my chest

And whisper into their ears

That they are safe

That there is nothing to fear

That I'll keep them safe

And in a few moments they're okay

If it wasn't for my babies

I'd never have heard those words

I so badly needed to hear myself

Words I was so desperate to hear from you

I told you I was haunted by demons

That I was afraid

I wish just once

You had held me

And told me

That I was safe

Fantasise

Some nights are so bad

I fantasise

I tell myself lies

Pretend you're here

You apologise

You don't shame my cries

Acknowledge how hard I've tried

I must be exhausted, you say

Sing me a lullaby

You smile

Refrain

I wish I had never complained

About my anxious heart and pain

Maybe then I wouldn't be

Standing alone in this rain

If I only did refrain

Maybe you wouldn't have said

I'm better off without you

Your words playover in my head

I deserve better

But I don't deserve

Your effort or changed behaviour

Your Song

I wish I could be strong

Move on

Perhaps I like pain

It's familiar, the same

Is that why my heart

Is stuck

Still singing your song

Saying that we belong

Righting every wrong

Reality Testing

Some days, some nights

I pretend you're still here

My reality testing is impaired

I remind myself

Your absence is just a figment of fear

I'm just *paranoid*

Your voice rings in my ears

You're true to your word

You're just around the corner

I tell myself

You're near

Replay

I replay our memories, like a movie in my mind

Was I happy? Were you kind?

Why do I subject myself to this taxing toll

When you were intent to show me I wasn't whole

Pretence

If I keep pretending that I'm okay

That's everything fine, that it's a sunny day

Will this nightmare I'm living fade into dust and die?

Even the pretence is painful, I can barely sigh

Your Side of the Bed

I look to your side of the bed, longing for your touch

Was I high maintenance? Did I ask for too much?

Your scent still seems to linger in the air

In this room where love we once shared

Scorpion Sting

Didn't I do the right thing?

By communicating through the fighting?

By being honest about how I was feeling?

By acknowledging the rupture and focusing on the healing?

Was my silence the only thing that kept you from fleeing?

What is it about my voice that is so unappealing?

Was it that it rang with words that needed your accounting?

Why does love have a scorpion sting?

All Roads

All roads lead me back to you

The people I meet

The things I do

How can I fight the World's reminders of you

When not long ago, my whole world *was* you?

Perhaps

Perhaps I wouldn't have been insecure

If you had provided me with security

Perhaps I wouldn't have feared infidelity

If you hadn't told me you couldn't help it if there was any

Perhaps I wouldn't have been the anxious mess you discarded

If you hadn't given me reason to be

Grand

All I wanted was to make it work

I communicated that I was hurt

It was so easy for you to hurt me

You did it thoughtlessly and effortlessly

But you were appalled at the idea

Of having to take accountability

It didn't matter to you

Though my pain was in full view

You made it clear to understand

That you didn't want me, and that's grand

But I'm stuck firm on this ground I stand

My heart is lost in wonderland

My love for you cannot be hanged

Cold

Creaking floorboards torment my wretched soul

As I pick up my broken pieces and try to make myself whole

Unforgiving winds chill my weary bones

It is cold, this place I call home

Mango Showers

It's summer again now

And it rained for the first time today

Mango Showers

Do you remember the time when we were lovers?

At the Door

Every sound and sight ignited hope inside
My primed body and teary eyes
It's you at the door
Eager to apologise
In my head I rehearsed my lines
A hundred times, and then some more
"You're always forgiven in this heart of mine"
"You have nothing for to apologise"
"None of that matters, I'm just glad you're here"

That I'd reject you, you didn't ever need to worry
You'd never a day live with insecurity
But the silence grew louder, tormenting my plea
I waited, I prayed that you'd come back to me

Every sound I heard, I hoped would lead to your embrace

You'd realise our love was worth another chase

Hope, a cruel fiend, danced in my heart

I yearned for the day

When you'd come knocking

And I wouldn't have to beg you to stay

But time ebbed away, and still you didn't appear

I saw myself drown in an open floodgate of tears

I keep finding ways to crucify my tireless heart

How is there anything left for me to tear apart?

Signs

There were so many coincidences

So many signs

In our lives and stories

I was convinced

The Universe was telling me

That it was written in the stars

You were mine

Our love, devine

The Devil

I saw the devil he was garlanded and grand

I approached him head-on with a valiant stand

For that which doesn't kill surely does weaken

Every battle I walked into feeling already beaten

Pulverised

I wish I had more pride

Had more self-respect and was dignified

But instead I tried, and cried

I was pulverised

Questions

How does one cope

With the reality

Of not mattering at all?

How does one

Get back up

After watching dreams fall?

Die on that Hill

You invalidated me

At every opportunity

"Do you want to die on that hill?"

You'd say

When my anger and hurt was rightful

And I'd disengage, be still

Let the emotion eat at me

Rather than let it pass through me

You've gone to war for less

Are we playing checkers or chess?

In Present Time

These months have been the test of my life

Terrifying, petrifying, so full of strife

The fear that as a child I refused to feel

Suddenly in present time it all felt so real

Curse

I carry so much hurt and pain

But still love you like I'm insane

Like you're the only person in the universe

Is there a way to break this curse?

Discard

I was whole when you found me

I was enough when you found me

You enjoyed me when you found me

So why did you break me down

Into little pieces

Into dust

Into something that you could so easily

Discard

Infidelity (i)

Disliking infidelity made me a prude

Faithful monogamy was too vanilla for you

Infidelity (ii)

Saying you wouldn't mind if I did it too

Is an appropriate response to infidelity to you

Infidelity (iii)

You say your friends have the same opinion as you

And so my pain gets no regard or due

Boy Scout

Rather than act like

A boy scout should I have

Let you slut me out?

Sorrow

In my desperation I have turned to astrology and taro,

I am a scientist who knows real sorrow.

Hate

They say there's a thin line between love and hate

You crossed over, sealed our fate

I think I've made a habit of being late

I still can't even see the line, is there a gate?

I don't switch sides, I contemplate

I take my time, let my feelings percolate

I remain unmoved, desolate

I hyperventilate

I overcompensate

I meditate

Withmyself I renegotiate

But I cannot bring myself to hate

Light

What do you see when you close your eyes?

Can you hear my cries?

Do you sleep at night?

Are there demons you fight?

You are at peace, you are light

Imagine

You said the effort of having to consider my feelings

Was too much and broke our dealings

Your actions so thoughtless and effortless

Destroyed my world, left me eternally screaming

Imagine what you could do

If you put your mind to it

Imagine what you could do

The Great Wall

I fell further down than I thought I could fall

Body so broken, all I could do was crawl

Do you think about me at all?

Between us you've built the greatest wall

Temporary

When I'm come undone

When it seems this can never be overcome

When I find myself wishing I had a gun

I try to remind myself

That this is just temporary

Everything is temporary

Fuck, that's scary

Healing

One of the most frustrating aspects of healing

Is that it is not linear

I think I might be moving on

And then find myself wishing you were still near

Never long enough living in lucidity

Before I find myself slipping back into fantasy

I'm glad you aren't floundering like me

I've never been much to envy

Except when you were with me

I do

"I don't believe it was that bad"

You said

When I told you everything that I had

As a child had experienced

At the hands of my family

I trusted you with the truth and my vulnerability

And was hurt more than ever before

I'd never felt so sore

I only deepen the wounds

By still loving you

I do

Never Had a Chance

It's been a year since we last spoke

The dust has settled, as has the smoke

I've imagined speaking with you a thousand times

I've thought of all the different things I could say

But despite these conversations being in my head

And all the variables being controlled in my stead

I still get it wrong, every single time

You react to feelings like I've committed a crime

If I can't get it right

In my own head

If I'm afraid and anxious to talk with you

In my own head

I guess

I never had a chance

With you

No Rest For The Wicked

I'm six feet under

But I hear the thunder

I feel the hurricane

The torrential rain

The pain

Is it because I'm wicked

That I get no rest

Even when I feel dead?

Unfold

You left me feeling alone and unworthy of care
Fearing my own mind, thoughts unfair
Not trusting myself, doubting my worth
Telling myself I've earned this curse

The burden of trauma, heavy and deep
Feeling like a failure, drowning in defeat
Shaming myself for self-pity's hold
Aching for validation, to break free and unfold

Providence

You told me everything that I lacked

And I accepted your word as gospel, as fact

You stripped me of my self-esteem

You were kind, so casually mean

I was left a wreck, with in myself no confidence

Your gift of holy providence

You filled my soul with doubt

Planted the seeds for demons to sprout

Afraid of the world, my shadow, the memories in my head

You left me wishing that I was dead

Legacy

A Masters degree in psychology

Hundreds of hours of therapy

Prescription drugs, not one but many

Fear, pain, insanity

The legacy you left me

Statistic

Pressure to be dead, a statistic so stark

Every therapy and medication, nothing hit the mark

Body and mind weathered by a malevolent tide

You were my emergency contact, but weren't by my side

Second Best

I lost my soulmate, trust shattered complete

I longed for connection which seemed an impossible feat

Haunted by a poltergeist that danced on my chest

I was never your priority, not even second best

Sheep

I admit the fault was mine

For believing love to be divine

For believing love to be more than a word

For believing I wasn't just another sheep in a herd

Where Was The Love?

You stripped me of all
My essence and then declared
That I wasn't enough

I was left with no
Perseverance or strength to
Fight when times got tough

And thus fulfilled the
Dictums you laid down and I
Ask where was the love?

You Didn’t Need to Shout

The hurt you dealt out

You were cruel, you didn’t need to shout

You’d make me cry and then just go about

Your day, like there wasn’t anything to clear out

Tidal Waves

You had me suicidal

And yet I believe you're ideal

You're on a pedestal, you're an idol

The waves that lash me are tidal

Advocate

I admit it's fair

For you to not care

Why do I advocate

For the person who made me need to medicate?

Why do I forsake my life

And invite your knife?

Logic

I used to think I had logic on my side

And so the truth was in view, there was nothing to hide

But you cut me off from my faculties when you left me behind

I wasn't just battered and bruised, I was blind

Minimised

I minimised my past traumas

Because you didn't like to hear about it

I invalidated and gaslit myself

To keep you from leaving

You left anyway

I Know You

I know you

Every colour, every hue

All the devious things you do

And yet for you I'd stand the queue

Knowing nothing would change or be new

Dismantled

You disregarded everything I said
Contradicted every thought in my head
You dismantled my ability
To think autonomously

Even if I said that the sky was blue
You'd tell me that that wasn't true
The security cameras recorded the break-in
I was terrified but you insisted I was mistaken

Everything I saw with my eyes
I was convinced was my mind telling lies
Everything that ran through my mind
Was automatically wrong, you defined

I feared losing my sanity

Feared I was losing my grip with reality

I wanted to die

And you were ready to let me

Stubborn

Love is stubborn

It doesn't flinch from a burn

It doesn't seem to learn

It doesn't want to turn

Away from You

Regret

I regret the vulnerabilities I shared with defile

Each trauma reminder causing a retraumatized mile

Simultaneously stuck and falling apart

I blame myself, for I saw this at the start

Body Count

What was it about your body count

That was so paramount?

You called them 'riff-raffs'

Did they have everything I lacked?

Toxic

You called me toxic

Said that I made you feel guilty

Intended only to make you unhappy

Because I shared with you my vulnerability

Told you how your actions hurt me

You called me toxic

So I set you free

Part II: Progress

At the Door (Pt. 2)

I accepted the truth, that you will never return
With memories of love that had brightly burned
The sound of raindrops upon the window pane
Echoed my tears, a testament to my endless pain
Every sound I hear, now holds a different story
Strength and resilience, amidst life's bitter glory

Every sound I *heard* I hoped was you at the door
Yearning for the day when our love could restore
You never knocked, offering your apology
I embraced the solitude, and set my spirit free
In each passing sound, a newfound grace
A reminder that self-love is the ultimate embrace

Dear Demon

To the demons that plague me I declare with fire

Your lies and pretence are not welcome here

To see your real self I know how much you fear

The very prospect brings to your eyes the elusive tear

In this land you can't escape the truth and disappear

You should probably ask for help, Demon dear

For I am now switching up the gear

You don't want to be near

For I now have my saviour

I'm here

Fear not, My Heart

Fear not, my heart, you're steel forged through fire

Embrace the scars and learn to rise higher

For when the storm passes, as it surely must

You may even find a heart that you can trust

I Love Being Wrong

I've gone so long

Without any contact

And I survived

Though I was so sure I wouldn't

I love being wrong

Perhaps

I can fulfil my lifetime

Without any sign

Of you

And I'll be just fine

For Me

I want to be proud
For not being afraid to say aloud
Everything that wasn't allowed
My contraband thoughts
My famine and drought
My unwavering love
I try not to shame
I will reclaim my heart
I'll keep picking up the pieces
I'll give myself another start
I'll see myself as marvellous
I'll see myself as art
I'm not for everyone
I wasn't for you
But
I can be enough
For me

Have it All

I loved you through it all

I loved you as you watched me fall

But

Love will help me stand tall

I have so much love in me

I can't wait for someone to have it all

Salvation

This desolation

Is my world, my creation

It must be then

That it is I

Who holds the key

To my salvation

Shadow Days

I've faced shadows that clouded my sunny days

But I found strength through the darkest haze

Fear lurked in the shadows, whispering its lies

Tempting me to surrender, giving teary cries

Yet with each ache and ache, I refused to fall

For courage within me stood tall, standing tall

The pain, oh, the pain, agony in its might

But I gathered my strength, I put up a fight

I was battered and bruised but unbroken

Not made any stronger even by a token

These months have tested the depths of my soul

But in the face of adversity, I've taken control

For within every dark night, a dawn still awaits

In the echoes of hardship, triumph resonates

But I emerge now, a phoenix ablaze

Ready to conquer life's ever-changing maze

A Cry in the Darkness

Oversharing, overthinking, a tangled mind

Wishing for respite, some solace to find

Caught in the storm of my own despair

But still hoping, despite the weight I bear

Forgive my ramblings, this torrent of woes

Aching for release, hoping someone knows

In these words, my pain finds its release

A cry in the darkness, a call for peace

Animals

Not one dog but three

Twenty more on the street

The three cats that visit me daily

The animals saved me

They showed me what love could be

They healed the insecurity you gifted me

They broke the shackles, they set me free

Out of Sight

Out of sight, out of mind

That would be merciful, that would be kind

But you are a part of me

You are in everything that I see

Perhaps forever, this will be

I Will Survive

With my dogs I'm not alone

With them around this place feels like home

I have a family, I have my tribe

It's a feeling of love and safety I can't describe

I was once blind but I don't need a scribe

This feeling is one you can't buy or bribe

It's the feeling that tells me I will survive

www.ingramcontent.com/pod-product-compliance
Lightning Source LLC
LaVergne TN
LVHW041059150826
845673LV00007B/1841
* 9 7 9 8 8 9 4 4 6 5 6 4 7 *